LOVE'S PROMISE

Love's Promise

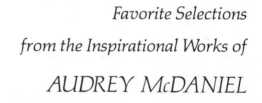

Favorite Selections

from the Inspirational Works of

AUDREY McDANIEL

Floral Designs by Hazel Hoffman

Doubleday & Company, Inc., Garden City, New York
1980

Library of Congress Cataloging in Publication Data

McDaniel, Audrey.
    Love's promise.

    1. Christian poetry, American. I. Title.
PS3563.A27A6 1980   811'.54   79-8935
ISBN 0-385-15607-3
Library of Congress Catalog Card Number 79-8935

First Edition
All Rights Reserved
Printed in the United States of America

May the love of God, which is from everlasting to everlasting, fill this collection from cover to cover, and may your hope be strengthened through faith in His love as you read each page. For it was written under the inspiration of God during shut-in days of illness. All credit belongs to Him for turning those shut-in days into a mission tied with a golden cord linking heaven and earth to His great heart.

I came to understand that God in His supreme intelligence weaves a perfect plan for each of us, and if we will seek Him with all of our hearts, He will lovingly grant an answer to our prayers, more wonderfully than we would have known to ask for. When I realized there was hope for every heart that employed faith, I begged God to use my life to help the less fortunate, the ill and the lonely — with no idea of what God would do with me — and I implored Him to go with me in the highways and byways to tell them He is Love.

In His miracle plan, this collection was conceived and forever each word in it shall be to His honor and glory, for I felt like only His secretary as I recorded these words in my several inspirational books, *Forget-Me-Nots of Love, Garden of Hope, God Is There, A Christmas Rose,* and *Abiding Love.* My own heart was so overcome and inspired by His love that I asked God to tie these words with His very own blossoms in moving sentiment befitting His promises that would stand eternally. And God did hear my prayer and did go with me every step of the way, as expressed in this collection, and He will forever be to me the talent, the loving agent in extending my work.

May the sacred theme of these pages fill your heart to overflowing with hope through faith in God's love, as Jesus taught me in those diamond interludes we spent together in my illness. God's love is not complex, not the unreachable star, but one love for all mankind.

Please believe me, my dear reader, when I say that this collection is for you from God with love, a treasured keepsake of lasting promises of hope through faith. And with Christ being the one perfect rose of all creation, it is lovingly tied together for you with roses.

LOVE'S PROMISE

"He gave us a Promise . . . . ."

WHO IS YOUR GUEST?
Hebrews 13:2

Be not forgetful to entertain strangers: for thereby some have entertained angels unawares.

BRING THE ROSES INDOORS:

Fill thy rooms with happiness. Carpet thy floor with roses that have been gathered in word or deed with dear ones. Add thy graciousness, thy mercy and thy concern for all who enter.

Encourage a prayer to bloom here reflecting, ". . . If ye have judged me to be faithful to the Lord, come into my house, and abide there . . ."

Acts 16:15

We ask for God to come to our door
And yet we forget the weary and poor
When we answer their knock upon our
    heart
God is our guest right from the start.

SOMEWHERE ALONG THE WAY

When some sad heart I met today
Did I use prayer to show the way
When some weary soul sore oppressed
Needed love to find peace and rest
Was I the one to say the word
Or leave them hurt and unheard
Did I have courage down in my heart
Enough to give them a brand new start
Was there patience ample for two
Did I care as I ought to do
Or did I see them walk away
Without sharing His Love today.

"He gave us a Promise . . . . ."

TWILIGHT:
Revelation 22:5

And there shall be no night there; and they
need no candle, neither light of the sun;
for the Lord God giveth them light: . . .

REST WHEN EVENING FALLS:

The nocturnal King of Night lighted the
Heavens with His golden torch and Eve-
ning, as if loathe to leave the beautiful
scene, pulled her curtain down and pinned
it with a Star.

Close your eyes and put your heart at rest.
In order that the new day may be more
dedicated to God, ask thyself at daytime's
closing hour, "What have I done for Thee
this day?"

As I lay me down to sleep
Heavenly Angels guard may keep
God's Love the canopy o'er my head
Peace of soul shall blanket my bed.

"He gave us a Promise . . . . ."

A RAMBLING ROSE:
Mark 6:56

And whithersoever he entered, into villages, or cities, or country, they laid the sick in the streets, and besought him that they might touch if it were but the border of his garment: and as many as touched him were made whole.

THE GREATEST LOVE STORY OF ALL:

Strolling through the New Testament with that sweet Teacher of Galilee, we find Him always busy about His Father's work. As He talks with the Twelve, pearls drop from His Lips; words of wisdom to be graven on the hearts of men.

Footsore and weary going to the sick and the needy, the just and the unworthy, ministering to all He met along the way.

Concluding His faithful service upon the Cross that there might be HOPE and ETERNAL LIFE for all He called His friends.

Dusk with soft shadows falling
At the quiet close of day
Moments of meditation
When I turn to God to pray
There in the evening silence
I ask my Father above
Please hear my earnest pleading
Watch o'er Thy people with love
Strengthen their faith dear Father
Bless them each step of the way
Then grant them peace in sleep Lord
Thy sweet Amen of the day.

13

MAKE ME A FRIEND

My friends from God will always be
Like petals of a rose to me
Each heart a pearl, each one a prayer
Wafted on earth's fragrant air
I thank Thee God for them each day
I'll try to understand their way
Listen to their secrets too
And never tell a soul but You
More important than the rest
I would have them love Thee best.

"He gave us a Promise . . . . ."

GOD'S GARDEN:
Isaiah 51:3

. . . like the garden of the Lord; joy and gladness shall be found therein, thanksgiving, and the voice of melody.

THE MASTER ARTIST:

Lift up your heart. In every niche, your life has love tucked in.

God, in His infinite artistry, created a beautiful Dresden-like setting for you to find peace unto your soul; with His vast expanse of palest blue o'er head, the pink accent of fragrant blossoms and the white representing the purity of His Holy Example.

The whispered affection of a loved one, the soft note of a downy bluebird and the inspiration of a sacred hymn bespeak the beauty He designed to help you and to put your heart at rest.

BECAUSE
THY LOVE IS NEAR

I thank Thee Father for Thy Love
Revealed to me from Heaven above
In sounds of laughter, fragrant air
In all the comfort of Thy care
Let all the deeds my life may do
Be something God that pleases You.

"He gave us a Promise . . . . ."

Be still, and know that I am God: . . .

FROM TEARS TO SMILES:

There is a Divine Mission in every heart-break. The disappointments we experience only tend to turn us to God.

These sadnesses are only an interruption of our happiness that we may come to know Him, not just about Him, and then we will never want to leave Him realizing all of the hours He has faithfully gone through with us.

As the cares of life send us to Him, time and again, we learn there is no heartbreak His Love cannot heal.

MY DEAREST LOVE

The hours I spend with Thee Dear God
Intrigued by love so true
The magic of the spell You weave
To keep me close to You

I find in Thee my Dearest Friend
A tender, gentle care
I could not make my way in life
Unless my plans You'd share

For Thou art all the things I need
The Love I seek in prayer
A rainbow's peaceful, Dresden hue
To tell me You are there.

"He gave us a Promise . . . . ."

O ANGEL OF THE GARDEN:
1 Peter 1:24, 25

. . . The grass withereth, and the flower thereof falleth away: But the word of the Lord endureth for ever . . .

LIKE A ROSE:

This beautiful life likened unto the Rose of Sharon. Rising early in the morning as the Petals of a Rose unfurl, dew kissed by God's Love — to sanctify another day — to bring another life to happiness.

So blossomed this GREAT HEART for others — permeating the fragrance of righteousness — breathed into the hearts and souls of men.

The Sacred Rose that softened a tear — THE ONE ROSE.

THIS LOVE OF JESUS

In every prayer He made to heaven
He asked for LOVE for you
Sought HOPE to ease your every care
With faith and comfort new.

And when a cruel and empty tomb
Turned radiant with His Love
I knew He bought the things for you
That had been planned above.

That HOPE He left within your heart
To live your whole life through
O Saviour, Hope of all mankind
Our loving thanks to you.

"He gave us a Promise . . . . ."

PRAYER, LIKENED UNTO A WEAVER:
Romans 8:25

. . . then do we with patience wait . . .

AT THE LOOM:

Prayer is likened unto a weaver sitting at a loom. We pray for something very expedient in our lives or for some one we love.

Days pass — no change — the colors on the loom are drab and grey and no pattern is discernible.

Suddenly, we see our prayer unfolding. The PATTERN ON THE LOOM takes shape and form. Be patient — wait.

GOD IS THE WEAVER, He sits at the loom.

GUIDANCE

My Father knows the way
    I cannot see
Within His Hands
He has a Gift of Love
    for me
So I will ever pray
    with open plea
For He will know what
    is the best for me
Not chain His Hands
Or ask for something
    planned by me
But trust My Father
For the things I cannot see.

"He gave us a Promise . . . . ."

WE NEED NEVER WALK ALONE:
Hebrews 13:5

. . . I will never leave thee, nor forsake
thee.

SIDE BY SIDE:

He longs to:
be part of our plans and lead us in the way
everlasting — search our hearts and know
our thoughts — shelter and sanctify —
in this togetherness.

If we were absolutely alone in this life, His
Love could suffice to fill our every need as
He is the only ULTIMATE LOVE of perfect
balance.

He is our LOVING COMPANION and GUIDE and
will not forsake us on the way.

TAKE EVERY DREAM

Take every dream within your heart
To God who really cares
He longs to hold you in His Arms
He listens for your prayers

Take every sigh and every tear
To Him who understands
Exchange these things for lasting peace
Within His loving Hands.

. . . and the desert shall rejoice, and blossom as the rose.

Isaiah 35:1

*   *   *

Sometimes, God has to use real discipline in love to cause us to follow Him.

We must remain in silence and listen as God conveys His will to us.

It is then we come into flower . . . and blossom in beauty of soul.

We shall not ask that the seeds of our lives be sown in a placid spot of our own choosing . . . but rather in a place where we may blossom more fully to please God.

How wonderful to know that the reflection of our lives can be a lamp unto our brother's path . . . a spiritual glow projected to the honor and glory of God, if we walk in Christ's footsteps.

* * *

For the LORD God is a sun and shield: the LORD will give grace and glory: no good thing will he withhold from them that walk uprightly.

Psalm 84:11

GARDEN OF LOVE

God came to the garden
   one cloudy day
And took all the worthless
   soil away
He nurtured the ground with
   His precious love
And then sent the showers
   so soft from above
Sacred blossoms then grew in
   this place
From the seeds of righteousness
   sown in grace
The garden attired like a
   heavenly dream
Now revealed His power
   and LOVE SUPREME

TEACH ME O LORD

Dear Lord with every passing day
Teach me to walk Thy sacred way,
And if my brother's path be dim
I'd like to be a light for him,
A candle on the darkest night
To chase the shadows out of sight
That opens up his eyes to see
The beauty of Thy majesty;
And then I'd ask along the way
That Thou would'st teach us how to pray
With open mind and open heart
Till all reveals HOW GREAT THOU ART.

There are no strangers . . . we are all friends through Jesus.

Our mission is to encourage these loved ones to render unto God the things that are pleasing to Him . . . to blend our souls with theirs to His honor and glory.

* * *

I pray for them: I pray not for the world, but for them which thou hast given me; for they are thine.

. . . Holy Father, keep through thine own name those whom thou hast given me, that they may be one, as we are.

John 17:9, 11

ALL FRIENDS FROM GOD

I'd like to know the peace He knew
As Jesus prayed when day was through,
How limitless such love could be
How tenderly He cares for me;
He told His Father up above
I have no one I do not love
Because I know that they were Thine
And by Thy love they now are mine.

When we abide in Jesus Christ there is a reason to look to the future with joy . . . a spiritual goal comes into view . . . new motivation for right living.

The patience of His understanding fortifies us to face the issues of life . . . suddenly the world around us becomes a PROMISED LAND.

*　*　*

Because thou hast been my help, therefore in the shadow of thy wings will I rejoice.

Psalm 63:7

WALKING WITH JESUS

When I am walking with Jesus
And Jesus is walking with me,
There's peace at the dusk of evening,
New visions of beauty I see;
There's hope in each morning sunrise
There's peace in His saving grace,
With such a dear Friend beside me
Talking face to face.

A haven of rest this friendship
As comfort and love fill the air
With Jesus so close beside me
Walking and talking in prayer;
With patience He understands me
So gently He holds my hand,
Tis then all the world around me
Is a promised land.

I pause as He offers forgiveness,
My heart with His love overflows
For peace like this in these moments,
The kind only Jesus bestows.
In my heart there's joy with Jesus
The cares of life fade away
So sweetly content beside Him
Walking there each day.

The Presence of Christ brings the peace that passeth all understanding.

Much of His ministry was dedicated to the broken in spirit, the halt and the lame.

He instilled in them this assurance . . . if they would abide in His love . . . no adversity could pluck them out of His hand. His generous heart sought to endow them with a serenity of soul that would give their lives HAPPINESS.

* * *

Thou wilt shew me the path of life: in thy presence is fulness of joy; at thy right hand there are pleasures for evermore.

Psalm 16:11

A WONDERFUL DAY

Twas a wonderful day in the garden
Because the Master was there
And I felt the glow of His presence
In the fragrance of the air
My heart turned to things of the spirit
My soul longed to sweeter be
In the gorgeous, righteous reflection
The nearness of Christ gave to me.

God is no part of heartbreak or disappointment. When the afflictions of the land beset us He would that His children COME UNTO HIM that He might ease their burdens and their joy be made full.

* * *

Casting all your care upon him; for he careth for you.

I Peter 5:7

. . . and God shall wipe away all tears from their eyes.

Revelation 7:17

GOD CARES

How could thy life be sad and drear
When all reveals that God is near
With heaven's blessings on thee falling
To tell thee that thy God is calling
In every thought and deed and prayer
Manifested everywhere.
Then turn in faith and feel the glow
Of love that wilt not let thee go,
The peace that only He can give
A reason for thy soul to live.
O wipe those tears from sorrowing eyes
God's love is streaming through blue skies.

God placed all children of His creation in a garden spot on this earth . . . enhancing each life with the beauty of His love.

He hung the celestial stars to light our eventide hours and He frosted the tender grass with pearly morning dew.

Would that our lives may ever preserve this sacred setting . . . and that our souls may add a fragrance of thanksgiving.

*   *   *

Every good gift and every perfect gift is from above, and cometh down from the Father . . .

James 1:17

WITH HIS LOVE

God placed a rose beside the wall,
Taught a bird to sweetly call,
Painted violets tender hue
Then gave them with His love to you.
He filled each buttercup with dew
In sweet communion passed anew,
Then lit a star with heavenly glow
To light our path on earth below.
He gave us hope for every heart
To give each one a brand new start,
Scattered friends along the way,
Blest and loved us as we'd pray;
O may some deed that we may do
Tell Him that we love Him too.

Just as God shall lavish the earth with wondrous splendor . . . clothe the lily in beauteous raiment . . . and give each tiny blossom its very own fragrance . . . how much more will He answer the longings of His children who walk in harmony with Him?

* * *

Consider the lilies of the field, how they grow; . . . shall he not much more clothe you, O ye of little faith?

Matthew 6:28, 30

GOD'S LOVING CARE

As the morning sun shall gild the skies
And His creation lift my eyes
As flowers on the earth appear
To manifest that He is near
As the shadows fall at the close of day
With its evensong and a time to pray
Tis a wondrous feeling to know that God
Secured each heart as this earth we trod
Just as a bird shall cease to sing
And tuck its head neath a feathered wing
Just as a rose shall petals close
And trust its God in sweet repose
So in our trials or burdens deep
God's love can give us peaceful sleep.

How wonderful to know that on life's highway Jesus will draw nigh unto us, if we seek Him with all of our hearts.

It matters to Him what our burdens are . . . He gave His all that we might know His love.

Then do not despair . . . THIS LOVE will not pass thee by.

*   *   *

The LORD upholdeth all that fall, and raiseth up all those that be bowed down.

Psalm 145:14

41

IF HE SHOULD PASS

If He should pass my way this day
And see me struggling as I pray,
If He should see my soul bowed down
Begging for a peaceful crown,
I know He'd stop along the way
And lift my burden as I pray;
I know that things would be made straight
As if He'd opened Heaven's gate.

Should clouds again bedim my sky
I'd seek once more this PASSER-BY
And say again abide with me,
For in Thy love is harmony.

In God's Garden of Hope there is one ROSE
. . . everblooming, the dearest of all His
creation . . . Jesus Christ.

A Saviour who speaks the language of love
all hearts are seeking and tenderly cares for
His own.

* * *

I will both lay me down in peace, and
sleep: for thou, LORD, only makest me
dwell in safety.

Psalm 4:8

THOU LORD ONLY

O put thy heart at rest in God
And in His safety dwell
For He alone doth hold thy hand
Thy future can foretell
So lay thee down in PEACE and SLEEP
And know that all is well.

. . . that we may lead a quiet and peaceable life . . .

I Timothy 2:2

* * *

God ever waits in the wings for His children's anxious prayer.

He is ever ready and willing to lift all burden and care.

If we will only pause on the highway of life to linger in this moment of sweet content . . . we shall become more mindful of our blessings and the peace that only He can give.

IN THE STILLNESS

In the chaos and the turmoil
Of life's very busy way
Will you pause for just a moment
There with God to kneel and pray
In the stillness and the silence
You will feel His Presence near
With the atmosphere so quiet
Words of Christ come to your ear
There you'll find a sacred haven
Where your weary soul shall rest
As the love of God surrounds you
Till you'll know that you are blest
He will understand your longings
Fill your heart with hope anew
In that precious, quiet place
Where God can speak to you.

And God saw every thing that he had
made, and, behold, it was very good.

Genesis 1:31

*   *   *

Since the beginning God planned a lovely
setting for His children . . . that their
souls might find peace and rest.

His Love for us is so personal. He did not
make the rose a thing of beauty just to por-
tray His artistry . . . but to beautify each
life.

He did not make man for the Sabbath . . .
but the sacred peace of the Sabbath . . .
for man.

It is all too easy to become so involved in
our own plans, that the blessings of God
are hidden from view.

A NEW START

Did I fail to see the sunshine
Or to hear the bluebird call
Did I count my many blessings
When God's love was over all
Had I closed my eyes to goodness
And the beauty of the day
How then could God still help me
When with thanks I failed to pray
Well, because He's ever faithful
Understanding, kind and true
He filled my heart with better
    thoughts
With these He let me start anew.

And Jesus said unto them, I am the bread of life: he that cometh to me shall never hunger; and he that believeth on me shall never thirst.

John 6:35

*   *   *

These promises from the sincere heart of Jesus Christ shall never fail us.

We may fail to keep our promises . . . but Jesus will forever fulfill His covenants with us.

When we turn to Him . . . He will lead us in paths of righteousness . . . and beside the still waters . . . where we shall not want. He will truly restore our souls.

Remember then, O weary heart . . . thou shalt never hunger . . . and never thirst . . . if He abide in our lives.

BESIDE THE STILL WATERS

I shall not want, I truly know
The Words of Christ have told me so
By waters peaceful, sweet and still
He will my every need fulfill
I know He'll never cast me out
For I can feel His love about.

O thou that hearest prayer, unto thee shall
all flesh come.

Psalm 65:2

*   *   *

Prayer is the silent conversation with the
great heart of God.

The golden cord linking heaven and earth
in these unspoken words.

The interlude of tranquility . . . as He ac-
cepts us . . . just as we are . . . and moti-
vates us to higher goals.

A resting place on the highway of life,
where one can linger from the world . . .
set apart . . . in peace.

Where all things are known to Him, and
yet, in His infinite mercy . . . forgiven and
blest.

SOMEONE WAS PRAYING

In the PRESENCE of the Master
Communing with Him there
I will place your name before Him
In my silent, sacred prayer

Then when you are with the Master
Offering up your silent prayer
Will you softly mention my name
For His BLESSING and His CARE.

. . . If I may touch but his clothes, I shall be whole.

Mark 5:28

*   *   *

We must lay our needs at the very hem of Christ's garment . . . where no good thing will He withhold from those who trust in Him.

As He manifested to the seeking cripple at the pool . . . when He asked him . . . are you willing to BELIEVE that I am able?

In this selfsame hour . . . as we pray BE-LIEVING . . . shall divine action take place.

. . . and great shall be the peace of thy children.

Isaiah 54:13

* * *

The problems of life may distress our hearts but the power of God is bigger than any storm we may encounter.

There is no storm that must not dissipate its course when God is in control.

It is a matter of faith in the crucial moments.

If we wander in despair, it is because we fail to call on the power of God.

LET FAITH ABIDE

O take God's Hand
  He's calling you
He offers help
  in all you do
Let not life's cares
  your heart dismay
God planned for you
  a better way

Then turn from fear
  Let faith abide
Your gracious Lord
  is by your side
Kneel down in peace
  and gently pray
For Jesus said . . .
  I AM THE WAY.

The eternal God is thy refuge, and under-
neath are the everlasting arms: . . .

Deuteronomy 33:27

* * *

Lift up your heart . . . in God there will
always be HOPE!

We are His very own and He really and
truly cares when shadows overtake us.

Life was not made for sorrow . . . and His
dear, precious LOVE can give . . . a sweeter
tomorrow.

MY LORD WAS THERE

When life's bleak burdens compassed me
And there seemed naught to set me free
'Twas suddenly my Lord appeared
And all the things my life had feared
Were lifted by His tender GRACE
His holy PRESENCE in this place
The sweet security of His LOVE
Had brought the peace of heaven above
The nearness of His PRESENCE too
Had brought me hope and faith anew
My life once more was sweet and fair
Because my precious Lord was there.

UNFAILING GRACE

I find the comfort for each care
Wrapped in a promise wondrous fair
No matter what the grief or pain
There will be sunshine after rain
A softest rainbow spans the sky
A symbol He keeps watch on high
We can never lose our way
If we abide in Him each day
Immortal LOVE through time to be
Is what He planned for you and me
Accept His help, turn not away
There is new HOPE in God each day.

. . . he hath sent me to bind up the
brokenhearted, . . .

Isaiah 61:1

*   *   *

Each life is ordained in the beautiful plan
of God to minister to those who are weak
and stumble in darkness.

To be a strong arm for the less fortunate
. . . and to witness to the faithfulness of
God in our own lives that we may encour-
age others.

To reflect . . . a GRACE sufficient for every
need.

GOLDEN HOURS

Fill each precious,
  golden hour
With some kindly
  word or deed
That will help
  a struggling loved one
Find the answer
  to their need
Let there be a pause
  of goodness
In each sacred,
  passing day
Blessed with joy
  we reap in serving
Those we meet
  along the way.

For ye shall go out with joy, and be led
forth with peace: . . .

Isaiah 55:12

*   *   *

The beautiful ministry of Jesus Christ was
accomplished to give us joy and peace.

He walked the rugged cobblestones to
patiently teach that in His Father's love
. . . was HOPE.

His entire life was dedicated to this end.
He viewed humanity with a burning desire
to deliver them from their burdens . . .
seeking no earthly praise . . . but minister-
ing, through love, to all He met.

And finally looking down from a cross . . .
forgiving and offering eternal life.

O PERFECT LOVE

Like the peace of prayer
  on stormy seas
Or a sacred hymn on an
  evening breeze
Is the comfort of God's
  precious Love
As He showers blessings
  from above
He offers mercy,
  compassion too
Forgives, as we confess
  the wrongs we do
Then sends us in peace
  on the road of life
With a promise to shelter
  in sunshine or strife
O what can I do
  to tell Him I care
And really say THANK YOU
  in solemn prayer.

All hearts are seeking
a Saviour who speaks
the language of love
and tenderly cares for
His own.

The sacred Rose that
eased all fear . . .

The One Rose . . . Jesus
Christ . . . who made a way
of Love for you and me.

This everlasting Love still
lights the world!

Think on these things.

We have never known a more
humble visitor or a more abiding Love
than that of Jesus The Saviour.

He ever stands at the door
of our hearts seeking to
enter. In the deepest of
humility saying—Let Me
come in and sup with you.

Just say you want Me . . . and I
will bring you all good gifts
from above.

I do not come to judge or
condemn but to love . . .
I am the way to the heart of
My Father in heaven.

THE MIRACLE OF LOVE

His Love is like a miracle
That sheds its grace and power
A hope for every weary heart
To light each precious hour
So ask your loving Saviour in
And bid Him never go
For He will listen patiently
And all His Love bestow.

The beautiful Season of
Christmas sprinkled the
earth with eternal promise
for all mankind.

Like fragrant blossoms
which fill the air . . .
the immortal words . . .
ring out to the world
the true meaning
of Christmas!

. . . Lord, to whom shall we
go? thou has the words of
eternal life.

John 6:68

Thanks be to God for the
teachings of Jesus Christ.

That real love will always
find a way to trust . . . through
confidence in God.

That in His perfection He made
the universe after His own heart.

And that all things work together
for good . . .

FOR GOD IS LOVE.

O Lord in all I do
    and say
I seek to serve Thee
    day by day
To sprinkle love, Lord,
    here and there
To wipe a tear and lift
    a care
And when each humble deed
    is done
To know that love has made
    us one.

Christmas is forever.

O to understand the mercy
of the healing Christ.

As they came to Him with troubled
hearts . . . He saw them
not in sternness
and rebuke . . . but as broken
lives in need of love.

And this ever compassionate
heart created within them a
new spirit and sent them on
their separate ways with the
beautiful . . . "Go in peace—
and the peace of God go with
you."

Lord let me build a dream
    of love
Through faith and trust
    in Thee
For everything Thou
    did'st create
Was perfect Lord for me.
Then let this dream of Love
    my Lord
Spill on the earth below
That through the channel
    of my life
Thy love will ever flow.

THE MATCHLESS JESUS

O Jesus how I ponder
Your matchless Love for me
And how my Father fashioned
A perfect Gift like Thee
The way you took my burden
And made it all your own
The most unselfish Love of all
The world has ever known
You'll not walk that road without me
As if I didn't care
For every time I needed you
I found your dear Heart there
I remember now your faithfulness
Your Love and Comfort too
So let me take your Hand dear Lord
And walk along with You.

As we celebrate the birth of
Jesus . . . in the warmth of candle
glow . . . the happiness of
friendships . . . the gifts of love . . .
may we be ever mindful of the
true meaning of Christmas.

For . . . Christmas unto Christmas . . .
shall be endowed with the divine
spirit of Christ Jesus.

Faith . . . hope . . . confidence . . .
and healing . . . but the greatest
of these is love.

The peace of God that passeth
all understanding.

And eternal life for those who
believe in God's priceless
Christmas Gift . . . Jesus Christ.

"O little Town of Bethlehem . . .
how still we see thee lie . . .
above thy deep and dreamless
sleep . . . the silent stars go by."

Thus the angels, the shepherds, the
wise men met in sweet accord.

For Christmas is the ultimate of
supreme gifts . . . the fulfillment
of total joy and hope.

"Fear not, only believe."

". . . and, lo, I am with you alway,
even unto the end of the world."

And these immortal words are the
Forget-me-Nots of the Christ Child.

Now as we deck the halls
    with holly
And hang the mistletoe
May our thoughts turn
    ever upward
To the God who loves us so
For the joys that make it
    CHRISTMAS
And its precious afterglow
Till our lives are one
    sweet Yuletide
As we serve on earth below.

Jesus came to confirm in the
earth . . . the precious Promises
of God.

*   *   *

And they shall be my people,
and I will be their God:

And I will give them one heart,
and one way . . .

And I will make an everlasting
covenant with them, that I will
not turn away from them, to do
them good . . .

Yea, I will rejoice over them
to do them good, and I will
plant them in this land
assuredly with my whole heart
and with my whole soul.

Jeremiah 32:38-41

THE ONE ROSE

A perfect Rose grew on the earth
In days of long ago
It had a special mission
As you and I both know
It came to earth a tiny Bud
With petals to unfold
That as they opened we might see
Fine jasper and rare gold
Its perfume gave a fragrance rare
Which souls may also do
If we will turn to God above
And to our Lord be true
Then as this Rose had opened wide
Its very heart to see
One knew this was the beauty
God sought in you and me
Then as its blooming ended
In quiet and sweet repose
God planned a further mission
For this One precious Rose
That in this world for you and me
One Rose would bloom eternally.

How often when burdened and in
deep despair has Jesus stayed
close by.

Faithfully sheltering us from
the storms of life that beset us.

Then as the clouds are lifted
through His patient, tender
Love . . . would that we put our
hand in His with a total
commitment.

Master, O faithful Love—
I'll go with you all the way!

Yes, I want to talk to you Lord
Of the things that trouble me
For I know that in your mercy
You can set my sad heart free
I should like to tell you Master
Of my grievances and shame
For I know your great compassion
Can redeem my soul from blame
I'd bare my hopes and
    dreams dear Lord
For your blessing and your grace
With my hand in yours my Saviour
Close beside you face to face.

Once we have come to an
awareness of Jesus' perfect
Love and His Spirit has
permeated our being — we then
long to be freed of self and·
become one in purpose with
Him.

It is then we seek to share
this fulfilling experience
with others as expressed in
the immortal words of Jesus.

*   *   *

. . . Holy Father, keep through
thine own name those whom
thou hast given me, that they
may be one, as we are.

John 17:11

TRULY ONE

As Christ lingered there
    beside me
With His comfort and His Love
I knew He was the dearest Gift
That came from heaven above
I bid Him tarry with me
Wished that He would never go
For my heart at last was happy
In this rare and sacred glow
All at once 'twas plain before me
And I knew the reason why
For the beauty of His Spirit
Filled all space of earth and sky
I believed in God the Father
And in Jesus Christ His Son
For the Love that filled these
    moments
Made us really, truly one.

Quietly . . . in majestic splendor
God lights His little heavenly
lamps — the tiny stars — in the
still of night.

To give us sweet repose and
illuminate our path below.

Likewise does His canopy of
Love enfold us every waking
moment.

Tender wings of security and
peace that cover our every
need.

* * *

. . . the earth is full of thy
riches.

Psalm 104:24

O then my dear Father . . .
As I gently pray . . . Send
my heart on a song . . . And
in service away.

Lord, give me serious things
to do . . . Things that hold
meaning just for You . . . Cause
me to ponder thoughts divine . . .
To please Thee, Lord, for I
am Thine . . . Lead me to those
in need of prayer . . . Help me
to show them Thou dost care.

*   *   *

Bless ye the Lord, all ye his
hosts; ye ministers of his,
that do his pleasure.

Psalm 103:21

85

INSTRUMENTS
FOR GOD

In your vineyard God I'd tarry
As an instrument of Thine
And I'd pray to heaven above me
That my life with love would shine
Ever seeking Lord to comfort
Those grown faint and weary too
Offering them a cup of water
As my Saviour bid me do
Use my life O precious Father
Let my Saviour lead the way
From the hours of the morning
Till at night I kneel to pray
Storing treasures up in heaven
Fruits of sacred deeds well done
Till I hear my Master saying
Child of God, we now are one.

Would that Jesus' Way of Love
permeate our very souls . . .
that in the faith of a little
child . . . we may come to know
His Way as one of simple
truth.

His divine ministry was based
on two things . . . to love . . . and
to believe.

For love believeth all things . . .
hopeth all things . . . endureth
all things . . . love never ends.

And love is rooted in faith,
through confidence in God.

Would that we come to accept
with our minds the things
we can understand and all other
things through faith in God.

SIMPLICITY

And though in wisdom
    I shall grow
And many worthwhile
    things shall know
No matter what my
    learning be
Lord, make a trusting
    child of me.

The first day of the week cometh
Mary Magdalene early, when it was
yet dark, unto the sepulchre, and
seeth the stone taken away from
the sepulchre.

Jesus saith unto her, Mary. She
turned herself, and saith unto
him, Rabboni; which is to say,
Master.

John 20:1, 16

*   *   *

If only our hearts would draw
nigh unto Jesus in devotion as
Mary did . . . we could then feel
the sacred impact of the true
garden experience.

Jesus had befriended Mary and
her life without Him was
meaningless.

But Jesus understood how sorely
she did grieve after Him and
appeared to her the very first . . .
So will He befriend all those
who turn to Him.

THE
EASTER
LOVE

I want to walk with Jesus
   every step of the way
To have His goodness sanctify
   each word I say
To follow Him through valley
To the mountains high above
Down every path, through
   every garden
To offer Him my love
To be like Mary Magdalene
Who walked with Him one day
Who felt such pain and anguish
When they took her Lord away
That Love so real appeared to her
When He her name did say
Then Mary found her peace of soul
When Christ stood there that day
He was her one true love you see
Like Mary may He walk with me.

The Peace of Meditation—

O Father, we treasure the moments
when we may stand before Thee in
deep silence.

In this atmosphere of serenity
and love . . . we shall come to
know that thy blessings are
resting upon us . . . and that
these diamond seconds are
filled with Thy Grace.

*   *   *

. . . and in this place will I give
peace, saith the Lord of hosts.

Haggai 2:9

PEACE SUPREME

Dear Father teach me this to know
In stress of life with hope dimmed low
That Thou canst weave a peace supreme
That is so real and not a dream
If in Thy arms we place each care
And understand that Thou art there
Then when our hearts with peace shall flow
To know our Father willed it so
Our anxious hearts to rest in Thee
Thou art our help eternally.

Let not your heart be troubled . . .

Jesus spent His entire ministry
trying to ease the heartbreak of
mankind . . . assuring us that in
every nook and crevice His Father
had placed symbols of hope.

Beyond the cloud . . . a rainbow.
For every tear . . . a smile.

No matter what the problem . . .
Jesus taught us that . . .
Faith in God the Father and in
Him . . . would give us a peaceful
solution to all things.

For faith leads to the secret place
of the Almighty, where in the arms
of His Love . . . we may find the
rainbow's end . . . contentment.

* * *

When my soul fainted . . . I remembered
the Lord . . .

Jonah 2:7

O Jesus how I treasure
Your perfect Love divine
To know that from my God
above
This Love is really mine
Thy dear, sweet calm
my soul doth fill
I know . . . Thy peace my
fears can still.